WHAT CAN IT BE?

Riddles About the Senses

Jacqueline A. Ball

Silver Press

Published by Silver Press, a division of Silver Burdett Press, Inc.
Morristown, NJ 07960

Printed in the United States of America.
10   9   8   7   6   5   4   3   2   1

Library of Congress Cataloging-in-Publication Data

Ball, Jacqueline A.,   Date.
Riddles about the Senses
p.   cm.   (What can it be?)
Summary: A collection of rhyming riddles describing sounds, tastes, colorful sights, and other sensations.
1. Riddles, Juvenile.   2. Senses and sensation——Juvenile humor.
[1. Senses and sensation.   2. Riddles.]
I. Title.   II. Series: Ball, Jacqueline A., What can it be?
PN6371.5.B28   1989   818'.5402——dc20

ISBN 0–671–68581–3   89–6384
ISBN 0–671–68580–5 (lib. bdg.)   CIP
ISBN 0-382-24388-9 (s/c)   AC

WHAT CAN IT BE? concept created by Jacqueline A. Ball

PHOTO CREDITS:
   Cover (clockwise from upper left): ANIMALS ANIMALS/Zig Leszczynski; EARTH SCENES/Richard Kolar; EARTH SCENES/ G. I. Bernard; ANIMALS ANIMALS/Doug Wechsler.
   Interior (in order of appearance): COMSTOCK/Hartman-DeWitt; Bruce Coleman, Inc./Lee Foster; COMSTOCK/Comstock; Barry L. Runk/Grant Heilman Photography; COMSTOCK/Comstock; COMSTOCK/David Lokey; COMSTOCK/Comstock; ANIMALS ANIMALS/Wilf Schurig; EARTH SCENES/Sydney Thomson; LeFever-Grushow/Grant Heilman Photography; ANIMALS ANIMALS/Zig Leszczynski; COMSTOCK/Jack Elness; Barry L. Runk/Grant Heilman Photography; COMSTOCK/Hartman-DeWitt; Barry L. Runk/Grant Heilman Photography.

BOOK DESIGN
   Cover: Helen Tullen, Nancy S. Norton
   Interior: Nancy S. Norton

Seven
Heavenly
Colors in a curve
That you only observe
After rain.

What is it?

A RAINBOW

Rainbows are the reflection of sunlight's seven colors: red, orange, yellow, green, blue, indigo, and violet. The colors are filtered through water droplets.

First, I'm in front.
Then, look out! I'm behind you.
Wherever you turn,
If there's sunshine,
I'll find you.
Sometimes I'm fatter,
Sometimes I'm thin.
But my shape doesn't matter.
I'm always your twin.

What am I?

YOUR SHADOW

A shadow is a dark place made when light is blocked by something solid. The length of a shadow can change depending on the time of day and where the light is coming from.

With a WHOOSH I'm let fly
Into darkness star-high.
BANG!
I shatter,
And scatter
Bright sparks in the sky
On the Fourth of July.

What am I?

FIREWORKS

Fireworks are
made from
gunpowder mixed
with metals that
add color. Only
adults should
handle fireworks—
they are
dangerous.

Feel the rhythm, hear the beat
Keeping time for marching feet.
Hear the trumpets, fifes, and flutes
Playing trills and tweets and toots.
See the sunlight's silver flash
As you hear the cymbals crash!

Now the soundshow starts to fade,
As down the street goes the ____.

PARADE

Some musical instruments have low sounds, like a bass drum. Some have high sounds, like a flute. All sounds become louder as they move closer to you.

When you want to be heard
In another location,
I send every word
Of your conversation—
From hello to good-by—
Over wires in the sky.

What am I?

A TELEPHONE

A telephone uses electric currents to carry sound. Your ears act almost like telephones that send sound messages to your brain.

If you have something
Secret to tell,
The voice
Of your choice
Should not be a yell.
Save for tomorrow
Sounds clearer and crisper.
To keep it
A secret,
Come nearer, and _____.

WHISPER

A whisper is a sound that's soft on purpose. If a sound is too soft, cup your hand over your ear. The sound will be funneled inside and you will hear it better.

I'm a soft, fluffy cushion,
A nest for your head.
I am found in fun fights
Or at rest on your bed.
Decked out in bright patterns
Or dressed in pure white,
I'm punchable,
Scrunchable,
All day and night.

What am I?

A PILLOW

A pillow feels soft and light because it is made of springy material like foam rubber or feathers. If a pillow were filled with sand, how would it feel? Why?

I come in all colors.
I grow first on birds.
You'll find my touch
Much too amusing for words.
So say, *Ha, ha,* and *ho, ho,*
Guffaw and *tee hee!*
You'll laugh yourself silly
When tickled by me!

What am I?

A FEATHER

When you stroke your arm with a feather, the tiny nerve endings under the top layer of skin start to vibrate. That's what makes you feel a tickle!

Not hot or cold,
But in between,
I'm where you soak
And scrub to get clean.
Use lots of suds—
But watch out for floods—
In your personal
Washing machine!

What am I?

A BATH

When you touch bath water that is too hot, the nerve endings in your skin send a message to your brain that says: *Ouch!* Your brain sends a message back: *Move your hand!*

My fragrance is sweet,
And my petals are fair.
But take care if you pick me—
I'm prickly!

What am I?

A ROSE

Roses and freshly cut grass are just two sweet outdoors smells. Like the salty smell of the ocean, they help you identify where you are and learn about the world.

By my stripe
You can tell
I'm the type
That can smell
Unbelievably bad—
When frightened
or MAD!

Phew! What am I?

A SKUNK

A skunk defends itself by spraying a bad-smelling liquid from a place near its tail. Other animals run away from the smell.

I'm round,
But I'm found
Packed up in a square.

When you free me,
All steamy,
My scent fills the air.

My slices smell nice—
Yum! Tomatoes and spice!
Don't you wish
You had ordered
A spare?

What am I?

A PIZZA

Heat can bring out the aromas in many foods, like pizza. Your sense of smell helps give you an appetite for the food you eat.

My white crystals twinkle
Whenever you sprinkle
Me over your golden French fries.
But use just a touch of me—
Using too much of me
Isn't too healthy or wise.

What am I?

SALT

Salt comes from the sea or beneath the ground. People use salt on food to bring out the flavor. The buds that taste salt are at the front and sides of your tongue.

What's the color of butter,
Bananas, and bees?

What's cut into wedges
For people's iced teas?

What isn't an apple,
But grows on fruit trees?

It's s-s-s-sour—
Use just a squeeze, please!

A LEMON

Lemons, pickles, and grapefruit taste sour. Taste buds on the sides of your tongue help you taste sour foods.

Green on the outside,
Pink within,
There's slurpy cool sweetness
Under my skin.
I'm the only dessert
Summer picnickers need,
So take a big bite!
Just don't swallow a seed.

What am I?

A WATERMELON

Watermelons, pineapples, and cantaloupes are all naturally sweet. Taste buds on the tip of your tongue help you taste sweet foods.